Chapter 1: Setting the Stage

Introduction to the Art of Hosting

Welcome to the exhilarating world of hosting, where every dinner party is a canvas waiting for your creative touch. Hosting is more than just preparing a meal and welcoming guests into your home; it's a craft, an art form that transforms ordinary gatherings into extraordinary experiences. In this section, we'll dive into the heart of hosting, exploring the essence of this delightful art and uncovering the joy it brings to both hosts and guests alike.

At its core, the art of hosting is about creating a space where people can come together, share stories, and forge connections. It's about the alchemy that occurs when good food, good company, and a welcoming environment combine to create magic. Think of yourself as the director of a play, with each dinner party as a unique performance. You set the stage, curate the cast (your guests), and guide the flow of the evening, creating an atmosphere that leaves a lasting impression.

As a host, you have the power to shape the entire experience, from the moment your guests walk through the door to the final toast of the evening. It's about crafting an environment that makes everyone feel not just welcome but truly appreciated. The art of hosting is in the details – the thoughtful touches that make your gathering stand out. It's the carefully chosen playlist that sets the mood, the personalized invitations that build anticipation, and the ambiance you create with lighting and decor.

But beyond the aesthetics, hosting is about fostering a sense of community. It's an opportunity to strengthen existing relationships and cultivate new ones. A well-hosted dinner party has the power to transcend the ordinary and create moments that linger in the hearts of your guests. It's an investment in the people around your table, a celebration of togetherness that goes beyond the confines of daily life.

In the chapters that follow, we'll guide you through the nuances of this art, from the initial planning stages to the final goodbyes. You'll discover how to navigate the intricacies of guest dynamics, choose the perfect date and time for your gathering, and curate a menu that reflects your culinary style. We'll explore the art of setting a captivating tablescape, sending invitations that excite, and facilitating conversations that flow seamlessly.

So, whether you're a novice looking to dip your toes into the world of hosting or an experienced entertainer seeking fresh inspiration, this chapter sets the stage for the exciting journey ahead. Get ready to unlock the secrets of the art of hosting, where every dinner party becomes a masterpiece, and you, the artist, are at the center of it all. Let the adventure begin!

Understanding Your Guests

As you embark on your journey into the world of hosting, one of the first and most crucial steps is getting to know your guests. Think of them as the co-stars in your dinner party production, each bringing a unique flavor to the ensemble. In this section, we'll explore the art of understanding your guests, helping you navigate the intricate dance of personalities and preferences that can make or break an evening.

Every group of guests is as diverse as a palette of colors, and your role as the host is to create a harmonious blend. Begin by considering the size of your gathering – an intimate dinner with close friends calls for a different approach than a larger celebration with a mix of acquaintances. Take a moment to reflect on the dynamics you want to foster – is it a cozy, familiar atmosphere or a lively and dynamic exchange?

Next, turn your attention to the individuals who will grace your table. Consider any dietary restrictions or preferences they may have. Are there vegetarians or vegans in the group? Any allergies or aversions to certain ingredients? Taking these factors into account not only ensures a pleasant dining experience for everyone but also demonstrates your thoughtfulness as a host.

Now, let's talk about the magic of guest dynamics. Consider the mix of personalities and how they might interact. Will the extroverts energize the room with lively conversation, or will the introverts appreciate a more intimate setting? Don't be afraid to play matchmaker with your guests, strategically seating them to encourage connections and spark interesting discussions.

As you contemplate your guest list, think about common interests and shared experiences. Finding common ground among your guests can serve as an excellent conversation starter and help bridge gaps between those who may be meeting for the first time. Maybe you have a couple of friends who share a love for hiking, or colleagues who both enjoy a good book – these connections, no matter how small, contribute to the overall warmth of the gathering.

Flexibility is another key when understanding your guests. While planning is essential, be prepared for the unexpected. Life happens, and last-minute changes are inevitable. Whether it's accommodating a surprise plus one or adjusting the menu to accommodate a sudden dietary restriction, a gracious host navigates these changes with ease, ensuring that everyone feels welcome and valued.

Ultimately, the art of understanding your guests is about creating an environment where each person feels seen and appreciated. It's about tailoring the evening to accommodate their needs and preferences, making them active participants in the experience. By taking the time to understand your guests on a deeper level, you set the stage for a night that goes beyond mere hospitality – it becomes a celebration of the unique tapestry of individuals gathered around your table. So, let's dive into the delightful dance of guest dynamics and create a symphony of connections that will resonate long after the plates have been cleared.

Selecting the Perfect Date and Time

The date and time you choose for your dinner party set the rhythm for the entire soirée. It's like selecting the perfect soundtrack for a movie – it sets the mood and determines the flow of the narrative. In this section, we'll unravel the art of choosing the ideal date and time for your gathering, ensuring that your dinner party hits all the right notes.

Begin by considering the nature of your event. Is it a casual weeknight get-together or a special celebration that warrants a weekend extravaganza? Understanding the purpose of your dinner party will help you gauge the level of formality and the ideal time to host. Weekends often provide more flexibility for guests to relax and indulge in a leisurely evening, while weekdays may call for a more streamlined and efficient affair.

Next, let's talk seasons. Each season brings its own charm and opportunities for thematic delights. A summer soirée could involve a sun-soaked backyard barbecue, while a winter gathering might feature cozy, candlelit ambiance and hearty comfort food. Consider the seasonal ingredients available for your menu and the overall atmosphere you want to create.

When pinpointing the date, be mindful of local events, holidays, and any potential scheduling conflicts. While hosting a dinner party on a major holiday might add a festive touch, it could also mean some guests have prior commitments. Check the local calendar, and if there's a significant event, embrace it as part of your theme or plan accordingly to avoid conflicts.

Now, let's talk timing. The hour you choose can significantly impact the mood of your gathering. An early evening dinner allows for natural light and lends itself to a more relaxed atmosphere. Meanwhile, a later start may set the stage for a sophisticated and elegant affair. Consider your guest list – are they early birds ready for a prompt start, or do they prefer a fashionably late entrance? Aligning your timing with the preferences of your guests ensures a smoother and more enjoyable experience for everyone.

Don't forget to factor in the duration of your dinner party. Are you envisioning a cozy, intimate gathering that wraps up early, or a lively affair that extends into the night? Communicate the expected duration on your invitations to help guests plan their schedules accordingly.

When selecting the perfect date and time, it's crucial to be considerate of your guests' commitments. A Friday or Saturday evening often offers more flexibility, but if you're aiming for a midweek gathering, consider a slightly earlier start time to accommodate work schedules.

Flexibility is the key to successful date and time selection. Life is unpredictable, and unexpected events may arise for both you and your guests. Be open to adjusting your plans if needed, and approach changes with a positive and adaptable mindset.

In the end, the perfect date and time are the ones that align with the vision you have for your dinner party and accommodate the schedules and preferences of your guests. So, as you navigate the calendar and clock, remember that the goal is to create an evening that flows seamlessly, allowing everyone to savor the experience without feeling rushed or constrained by time. Let the countdown to your unforgettable dinner party begin!

Chapter 2: Planning the Menu

Welcome to the heart of the culinary adventure: planning the menu! If hosting a dinner party is a symphony, then the menu is your composition, a melody of flavors that will dance on the taste buds of your guests.

In this chapter, we dive into the art and science of crafting a menu that not only satiates appetites but leaves a lasting impression. From selecting the right balance of flavors, textures, and cuisines to considering dietary preferences and restrictions, we embark on a culinary journey together. Get ready to explore the magic of pairing food and drinks, creating a cohesive dining experience that elevates your dinner party from ordinary to extraordinary.

So, put on your chef's hat, sharpen those knives, and let's curate a menu that will have your guests talking long after the plates are cleared. The stage is set, the kitchen awaits, and your culinary masterpiece is about to unfold. Bon appétit!

Crafting a Cohesive Menu

Welcome to the culinary canvas of your dinner party – where each dish is a stroke of flavor, and the menu, a masterpiece in the making. In this section, we'll delve into the art of crafting a cohesive menu, ensuring that each bite contributes to the symphony of tastes you aim to orchestrate.

Start by envisioning the experience you want your guests to have. Are you aiming for a casual and comforting affair, or perhaps a more formal and elegant dining experience? Understanding the overall theme and atmosphere of your gathering will guide your menu choices.

Consider the balance of flavors, textures, and cuisines. A well-rounded menu offers a variety of tastes that complement each other. If you're featuring a rich and hearty main course, balance it with lighter appetizers and sides. Think of your menu as a story with a beginning, middle, and end, where each dish seamlessly transitions to the next, creating a delightful narrative for your guests' taste buds.

Now, let's talk about variety. Incorporate a mix of proteins, vegetables, and grains to cater to different dietary preferences. A diverse menu not only accommodates various tastes but also adds visual appeal to your table. If you're feeling adventurous, experiment with international flavors, taking your guests on a global culinary journey without leaving the comfort of your home.

Seasonality is another key factor in crafting a cohesive menu. Utilize fresh, in-season ingredients to enhance the vibrancy and quality of your dishes. Not only does this approach support local farmers, but it also adds a touch of authenticity and captures the essence of the moment.

Consider the logistics of preparation. Aim for a balance between dishes that can be made in advance and those that require last-minute attention. This ensures that you're not chained to the kitchen throughout the evening, allowing you to enjoy the company of your guests.

As you brainstorm and curate your menu, don't forget to factor in any dietary restrictions or preferences among your guests. Offering options for vegetarians, vegans, or those with allergies demonstrates thoughtfulness and inclusivity. You want every guest to feel excited about the culinary journey you've prepared for them.

Once you have a draft of your menu, step back and review it as a whole. Does it tell the story you envisioned? Are there any gaps or redundancies? Adjust as needed to create a harmonious flow that builds anticipation from the appetizers to the grand finale.

In the end, crafting a cohesive menu is about intention and balance. It's about creating a culinary experience that mirrors the warmth and thoughtfulness you've put into every other aspect of your dinner party. So, roll up your sleeves, gather your ingredients, and let the creativity flow as you compose a menu that will have your guests savoring the magic of your culinary artistry. Get ready to embark on a gastronomic journey where every dish is a note in the symphony of your dinner party. Cheers to the delicious adventure ahead!

The Art of Pairing: Food and Drinks

Welcome to the flavorful dance of the dinner table, where the perfect pairing of food and drinks transforms a meal into a symphony for the senses. In this section, we'll explore the art of harmonizing flavors, ensuring that each sip and bite enhance the overall dining experience.

Begin by considering the primary elements of your dishes – the flavors, textures, and intensity. A robust red wine might complement a hearty beef stew, while a crisp white wine or a sparkling beverage could elevate a delicate fish dish. Pay attention to the dominant flavors in each dish and seek drinks that either complement or contrast, creating a delightful balance.

Think about the progression of your meal. If you're serving multiple courses, consider how the drinks transition from one dish to the next. Starting with lighter beverages for appetizers and gradually moving to more complex pairings with the main course allows your guests to explore a variety of tastes throughout the evening.

Don't limit yourself to just wine. Experiment with craft cocktails, mocktails, or even curated non-alcoholic beverages to cater to all preferences. The art of pairing extends beyond alcoholic options, and thoughtful choices in this realm can enhance the overall inclusivity of your dining experience.

Consider the seasonality of your beverages. Just like your menu, selecting drinks with seasonal ingredients adds an extra layer of freshness and authenticity to your gathering. A citrusy cocktail might be perfect for a summer soirée, while a warm mulled cider could be the ideal companion for a fall feast.

Guiding your guests through the pairing experience can be a delightful part of the evening. If you have unique or unfamiliar beverages, consider providing brief descriptions or even a small tasting note card at each place setting. This not only adds an educational element but also sparks conversations among your guests.

When in doubt, ask for expert advice. Many local wine shops or beverage specialists are more than happy to help you navigate the world of pairings. Share your menu and preferences with them, and they can recommend options that complement your dishes seamlessly.

Remember that personal preferences vary. While you can offer suggestions, encourage your guests to explore and find their own preferred pairings. Some may appreciate a bold red wine with their dessert, while others might prefer a sweet cocktail or a hot cup of tea.

The art of pairing is a journey of discovery and creativity. Don't be afraid to experiment, trust your instincts, and most importantly, enjoy the process. As you bring together complementary and contrasting flavors on your dinner table, you're not just providing sustenance – you're orchestrating a gastronomic experience that will linger in the memories of your guests. So, raise a glass to the art of pairing, where every sip and every bite contribute to the symphony of your extraordinary dinner party. Cheers!

Kitchen Tips and Tricks

Welcome to the heart of your culinary command center – the kitchen! In this section, we'll explore some kitchen tips and tricks to help you navigate the delightful chaos of preparing a menu that will dazzle your guests. From streamlining your cooking process to managing last-minute surprises, let's dive into the world of culinary wizardry.

Plan and Prep Ahead: A well-thought-out plan is your kitchen's best friend. Create a timeline for your cooking process, breaking down tasks into manageable steps. Consider what can be prepared in advance, from chopping vegetables to marinating proteins. This not only eases the day-of workload but also allows you to enjoy the festivities with your guests.

Embrace Make-Ahead Dishes: Certain dishes are even better when prepared in advance. Soups, stews, and many desserts often benefit from some extra time to meld flavors. Make-ahead dishes not only simplify your day but often taste even more delicious as the flavors have had time to develop.

Delegation is Your Ally: Don't hesitate to enlist the help of friends or family. Assign tasks based on individual strengths – someone might be a wizard with appetizers, while another excels at dessert. Not only does this lighten your load, but it also brings a collaborative and communal spirit to the kitchen.

Keep it Simple (But Elegant): While it's tempting to showcase your culinary prowess with elaborate recipes, simplicity can be just as impressive. Focus on quality ingredients and straightforward techniques. Elegant dishes don't always require a multitude of components; sometimes, it's the simplicity that allows each ingredient to shine.

Test Your Recipes: If you're trying out new recipes for the first time, consider doing a trial run. This ensures that you're familiar with the process and can troubleshoot any potential issues. It also provides an opportunity to adjust flavors to your liking and discover any hidden culinary gems.

Create a Mise en Place: The French culinary concept of mise en place, meaning "everything in its place," is a game-changer. Before you start cooking, organize and set out all your ingredients. This not only enhances efficiency but also prevents those frantic moments of searching for a crucial ingredient mid-preparation.

Label and Date: If you're preparing dishes in advance or freezing portions, label and date everything. This simple step can save you from the guessing game and ensures that you're serving the freshest dishes possible.

Stay Cool Under Pressure: Kitchen mishaps happen to the best of us. Whether you accidentally add salt instead of sugar or slightly overcook the main course, don't panic. Many kitchen mishaps have creative solutions, and sometimes these unexpected twists add a touch of charm to your culinary journey.

Invest in Quality Tools: A sharp knife, reliable cookware, and essential kitchen gadgets are your allies in the kitchen. Investing in quality tools can make your cooking process smoother and more enjoyable.

Enjoy the Process: Remember, the kitchen is a place of creativity and joy. Embrace the process, enjoy the aromas, and savor the satisfaction of creating a delightful feast for your guests. If things don't go as planned, laugh it off, and let the experience be part of the story you share with your guests.

As you embark on your culinary adventure, armed with these kitchen tips and tricks, remember that the most important ingredient is your passion for creating a memorable dining experience. So, apron on, spatula in hand, and let the kitchen magic begin!

Chapter 3: Mastering Tablescapes

Welcome to the creative hub of your dinner party – Chapter 3: Mastering Tablescapes! This chapter is where we transform your dining table into a visual masterpiece, setting the stage for an unforgettable evening. Much like a painter with a blank canvas, you have the power to craft a tableau that not only complements your culinary creations but also enhances the overall ambiance.

In the pages ahead, we'll explore the art of creating captivating tablescapes, from selecting the perfect linens and dinnerware to crafting eye-catching centerpieces that captivate your guests. Whether you're aiming for an intimate and cozy setting or a lavish and elegant affair, this chapter is your guide to turning your table into a work of art.

So, let your creativity flow, embrace the beauty of details, and get ready to master the art of tablescapes that will leave your guests in awe. The table is your canvas, and you are the artist – let's bring your vision to life!

The Importance of Ambiance

Step into the world of ambiance, where the atmosphere you create becomes the silent host of your dinner party. In this section, we'll explore why setting the right ambiance is like casting a spell, weaving an invisible thread that ties together all the elements of your tablescapes and elevates your gathering to a truly magical experience.

A Feast for the Senses: Ambiance is the secret sauce that turns a meal into a memorable event. It engages not only the sense of taste but also sight, smell, touch, and even sound. Imagine walking into a room where the soft glow of candlelight dances on carefully arranged table settings, the aroma of your favorite dishes wafts through the air, and soothing music creates a backdrop for conversation. That's the power of ambiance – it's a multi-sensory journey that enhances every aspect of your dinner party.

Lighting Magic: The right lighting sets the mood like nothing else. Consider the natural light streaming in during a sunset dinner or the warm, intimate glow of candles and string lights for an evening affair. Experiment with different light sources to create a play of shadows and highlights, adding depth and dimension to your table.

Music as a Companion: Music is the unsung hero of ambiance. Choose a playlist that complements the mood you want to establish – whether it's lively tunes for a festive gathering or soft melodies for an intimate dinner. The right music can fill any lulls in conversation and create a harmonious background for your feast.

Cohesive Themes: Ambiance and themes go hand in hand. Whether it's a seasonal theme, a cultural celebration, or a color palette that ties everything together, a cohesive theme adds a layer of sophistication to your tablescapes. It guides your choices in decorations, linens, and even the style of your dinnerware.

Consider the Seating Arrangement: Ambiance extends to the seating arrangement. Think about how guests will interact with each other. Round tables encourage conversation, while long banquet-style tables create a sense of communal feasting. Strategic seating can foster connections and make everyone feel included in the festivities.

Personal Touches: Inject a bit of your personality into the ambiance. Personal touches, like handwritten place cards, custom-made centerpieces, or even a curated selection of family photographs, add a layer of authenticity and warmth to your table.

Adapt to the Occasion: The ambiance you create should be tailored to the occasion. A casual brunch may call for a bright and airy setting, while a formal dinner benefits from a more refined and elegant atmosphere. Consider the purpose of your gathering and adjust the ambiance accordingly.

8. Flow of Energy: Think of ambiance as the energy that flows through your dinner party. A well-thought-out ambiance encourages guests to linger, engage in conversation, and savor the moment. It creates a positive and welcoming energy that ensures everyone feels comfortable and connected.

In the end, the importance of ambiance lies in its ability to transform your dinner party from a simple meal into an immersive experience. It's the intangible thread that ties together all the visual and sensory elements, creating a space where laughter lingers and memories are made. So, as you embark on the journey of mastering tablescapes, remember that ambiance is your ally, your co-host, and the enchanting backdrop to the culinary and visual feast you're preparing for your guests. Let the ambiance set the stage for an extraordinary evening!

Centerpiece Magic

Enter the realm of centerpiece magic, where the focal point of your table becomes a captivating storyteller, weaving narratives without uttering a word. In this section, we'll unravel the art of creating centerpieces that not only command attention but also infuse your table with personality, style, and a touch of enchantment.

The Heart of the Table: The centerpiece is the beating heart of your tablescape, and getting it right can elevate the entire dining experience. It's the anchor that ties everything together, providing a visual feast for your guests even before the first course is served.

Balance and Proportion: When selecting or creating a centerpiece, consider the size and shape of your table. A large, extravagant arrangement may overwhelm a smaller table, while a petite centerpiece might get lost on a grand dining surface. Aim for balance and proportion that complements the dimensions of your table.

Seasonal Flourish: Embrace the magic of the seasons with your centerpiece. Fresh blooms and vibrant greens in spring, sunflowers and warm hues in the fall, and perhaps a touch of sparkle for winter festivities. Seasonal elements not only connect your table to nature but also add a dynamic and ever-changing aspect to your gatherings.

DIY Delights: Creating a centerpiece can be a delightful DIY project. Whether it's a simple arrangement of wildflowers in mason jars or an intricate display of candles and driftwood, infusing your personality into a handmade centerpiece adds a unique touch. Consider the theme of your dinner party and let your creativity flow.

Height and Drama: Play with height to add drama to your centerpiece. Tall candlesticks, elegant vases, or suspended elements create visual interest and draw the eye upward. However, be mindful not to obstruct the view across the table, allowing for easy conversation.

Lighting Matters: Incorporating candles into your centerpiece not only adds a warm and inviting glow but also contributes to the overall ambiance. Consider pillar candles, tea lights, or even LED string lights intertwined with greenery for a magical touch.

Edible Elegance: For a whimsical and functional twist, consider incorporating edible elements into your centerpiece. A bowl of vibrant fruits, a selection of cheeses, or even a cascading display of desserts can double as both a visual feast and a delightful treat for your guests.

Theme Integration: If your dinner party has a specific theme, let it shine through in your centerpiece. Nautical elements for a beach-themed dinner, vintage books for a literary gathering, or miniature pumpkins for a fall feast – integrating your theme into the centerpiece adds cohesiveness to the overall design.

Conversation Starter: A well-crafted centerpiece becomes a conversation starter. Whether it sparks admiration for its beauty, prompts discussions about its elements, or simply serves as a point of connection among guests, a thoughtful centerpiece contributes to the lively energy around your table.

Versatility: Consider the versatility of your centerpiece. Can it be adapted for different occasions or themes? A versatile centerpiece allows you to reuse and repurpose, saving both time and resources for future gatherings.

In the realm of centerpiece magic, there are no rigid rules—only opportunities for creativity and self-expression. Let your imagination guide you as you curate a centerpiece that transforms your table into a visual masterpiece. With a touch of magic, a dash of personality, and a sprinkle of creativity, your centerpiece will enchant your guests, making every dinner party a feast for the eyes as well as the palate. So, embark on the journey of centerpiece creation, and let the magic unfold on your dining table!

Seating Arrangements

Take a seat at the planning table because we're diving into the art of seating arrangements! In this section, we'll explore the nuances of arranging seats to foster connections, encourage lively conversations, and ensure every guest feels like a VIP at your dinner party.

Intentional Pairings: Consider the dynamics among your guests when crafting your seating arrangement. Mixing extroverts with introverts can balance the energy, while placing friends with common interests side by side encourages engaging conversations. Think about who might spark interesting dialogues or enjoy each other's company.

Round vs. Rectangular: The shape of your table influences the flow of conversation. Round tables create an inclusive atmosphere, allowing everyone to see and interact with each other easily. On the other hand, rectangular tables offer a more structured arrangement, ideal for larger gatherings or formal dinners. Choose the shape that aligns with the vibe you want to create.

Head of the Table: If your table has a designated head, consider who will occupy this seat. Traditionally, the host or guest of honor sits at the head of the table, but you can also opt for a more democratic approach and have a seat rotation for different courses. The head of the table sets the tone, so choose wisely based on the dynamics you want to encourage.

Mix and Mingle: Don't be afraid to mix and mingle. A purely hierarchical seating arrangement may not suit every occasion. Consider a blend of formal and informal by interspersing family and close friends with colleagues or acquaintances. This creates a dynamic atmosphere and facilitates connections across different social circles.

Consider Comfort: Ensure ample space between chairs for comfort. No one wants to feel cramped during a leisurely dinner. A well-spaced seating arrangement allows guests to enjoy their meals without feeling confined and promotes a relaxed and enjoyable dining experience.

Name Cards: Name cards aren't just for formal events—they're a helpful tool for guiding guests to their seats and ensuring a smooth transition into dinner. Personalize them with a touch of creativity or tie them into your overall theme for an extra dash of charm.

Flexibility: Be flexible with your seating arrangement. Sometimes, guests may prefer or request specific seating, or unforeseen circumstances may prompt changes. A flexible approach ensures that everyone feels accommodated and valued.

Kids' Corner: If your dinner party includes children, consider creating a designated "kids' corner." Arrange seating to group them together, allowing the little ones to interact and have their own mini celebration. This thoughtful arrangement not only ensures the comfort of parents but also keeps the young ones entertained.

Visual Appeal: Think about the visual appeal of your seating arrangement. Experiment with different tablescapes, color schemes, or even unique chair arrangements to add a visual touch that complements your overall theme. An aesthetically pleasing setting contributes to the overall ambiance of your dinner party.

Lasting Impressions: The goal is to leave a lasting impression. Consider how guests will feel when they find their assigned seats. A thoughtful seating arrangement communicates that you've considered each person's presence and that their experience is important to you.

In the art of seating arrangements, every seat tells a story. It's about curating an environment where connections flourish, conversations flow, and everyone feels like an integral part of the evening. So, as you arrange the seats at your dinner table, let the art of connection guide you. Craft an arrangement that not only ensures a harmonious flow of conversation but also creates an atmosphere where laughter, camaraderie, and the joy of shared moments take center stage. Get ready to master the art of seating arrangements and watch as your dinner party unfolds into a symphony of connections!

Chapter 4: Invitations and Etiquette

Step into the realm of anticipation and courtesy as we explore Chapter 4: Invitations and Etiquette. This chapter is your guide to the art of extending the perfect invitation, creating the first chord in the melody of your dinner party. From the initial spark of inspiration to the graceful execution of RSVPs, we'll navigate the intricacies of inviting guests with warmth, style, and a touch of flair.

Join me as we uncover the etiquette that makes every invitation a gracious gesture and sets the tone for an evening filled with camaraderie and shared delights. Whether you're planning an intimate gathering or a grand celebration, this chapter is your invitation to master the art of extending hospitality and creating a welcoming atmosphere.

So, let's embark on this journey of politeness and charm, where every invitation becomes a prelude to the extraordinary feast that awaits. Get ready to send out the invitations that will have your guests eagerly counting down the days until your spectacular dinner party!

Crafting Invitations that Excite

Your dinner party begins long before the first dish is served—it starts with the excitement sparked by a well-crafted invitation. In this section, we'll explore the art of crafting invitations that not only inform but also enthrall, setting the stage for an unforgettable gathering filled with anticipation and delight.

The Prelude: Think of your invitation as the opening notes of a symphony, inviting your guests to join in the celebration. Begin with a warm greeting that reflects your personal style and sets the tone for the event. Whether it's a playful "Join us for a night of culinary adventures!" or a classic "You're invited to an evening of fine dining," let the language resonate with the ambiance you aim to create.

Theme Teasers: If your dinner party has a theme, drop subtle hints in the invitation. Whether it's a color scheme, a specific cuisine, or a unique dress code, incorporating theme teasers builds excitement and gives guests a glimpse into the experience you have in store for them. For example, "Dress in your favorite beach attire for a seaside soiree" or "Prepare your taste buds for a journey through Mediterranean flavors."

Unveil the Menu: For an added touch of anticipation, provide a sneak peek into the culinary delights awaiting your guests. Highlight a signature dish or share a tantalizing description of the menu.

This not only builds excitement but also allows guests to prepare their palates for the feast ahead. For instance, "Indulge in a decadent chocolate fondue finale" or "Savor the flavors of a five-course Italian extravaganza."

Creative Formats: Experiment with creative formats to make your invitation stand out. Whether it's an elegant paper invitation, a playful digital design, or even a themed video invitation, the format sets the stage for the event's style. Consider the tone of your gathering and choose a format that aligns with the overall aesthetic, leaving guests eager to experience the magic you've hinted at.

Practical Details with Style: While the excitement is paramount, don't forget the practical details. Clearly communicate the date, time, and location of your dinner party. Include any additional information, such as dress code or parking instructions. Infuse these details with your personal touch, ensuring that even the logistical information reflects the warmth and style of your event.

RSVP with Enthusiasm: Encourage a sense of involvement and enthusiasm in the RSVP process. Instead of a standard "Kindly RSVP," use language that sparks anticipation. Try phrases like "We can't wait to celebrate with you! Will you be joining us?" or "Count me in for a night of joy and laughter!"

Personalized Touches: Add personalized touches to your invitations, making each guest feel special. Handwritten notes, customized illustrations, or even a thoughtful quote related to the theme can elevate the invitation from a mere formality to a heartfelt gesture.

Timing is Everything: Send out your invitations with strategic timing. Aim for a balance—early enough to allow guests to plan, but not so early that the excitement wanes. Consider the nature of your event—a casual gathering may warrant a more relaxed timeline, while a formal affair might require more lead time.

Digital Dynamism: In the age of technology, leverage digital platforms for dynamic invitations. Create interactive invitations, complete with clickable RSVP buttons, animated graphics, or even a virtual tour of your venue. Embrace the versatility of digital mediums to add an extra layer of excitement.

Follow-Up Flourish: After sending the invitations, follow up with a flourish. A friendly reminder closer to the RSVP deadline not only ensures you get accurate responses but also reignites the excitement for the upcoming event. Use this opportunity to share a teaser or additional details to keep the anticipation alive.

Crafting invitations that excite is an art that combines practicality with creativity. Your invitation serves as the initial spark that ignites the anticipation, paving the way for a night filled with joy and shared experiences. So, as you put pen to paper or pixels to screen, infuse your invitations with the energy and excitement that make your dinner party an event to remember. Get ready to see the enthusiasm reflected in the eyes of your guests as they eagerly await the culinary extravaganza you've meticulously planned!

RSVP Management

Once the invitations are sent and the anticipation builds, it's time to dive into the dance of RSVPs. In this section, we'll unravel the art of managing RSVPs with grace and efficiency, ensuring a smooth journey from invitation to guest list and creating an atmosphere of excitement as your dinner party approaches.

Clear and Convenient Options: Make responding to your invitation a breeze by providing clear and convenient RSVP options. Whether it's a reply card, an email address, or a digital RSVP platform, ensure that the method aligns with the preferences of your guests. The goal is to make the process as straightforward and accessible as possible.

Online RSVP Platforms: Leverage the power of technology with online RSVP platforms. Websites or apps dedicated to event management streamline the process for both hosts and guests. They often include features like automatic reminders, dietary preference collection, and real-time guest list updates, making the RSVP experience efficient and user-friendly.

Set a Clear Deadline: Establish a clear RSVP deadline to give yourself ample time for final preparations. Communicate the deadline clearly in your invitation, and if possible, set it slightly earlier than needed. This provides a buffer for any last-minute adjustments and ensures you have a complete and accurate guest count well before the event.

Gentle Reminders: A friendly reminder nudges those who might have overlooked the RSVP deadline. Send a gentle reminder a week or so before the cutoff, expressing your excitement about their attendance. This not only prompts timely responses but also rekindles the anticipation for your upcoming gathering.

Flexibility with Plus-Ones: Be clear about your stance on plus-ones in your invitation, and, if applicable, provide guidelines. Whether you're open to guests bringing a date or prefer a more intimate affair, clarity on plus-ones helps manage expectations and avoids any potential confusion.

Gracious Handling of Regrets: Responses might include regrets, and that's perfectly okay. Respond graciously to those unable to attend, expressing understanding and conveying that you'll miss their presence. This fosters a positive connection and keeps the door open for future invitations.

Dietary Preferences: If your dinner party involves a sit-down meal, inquire about dietary preferences in your RSVP. Include a section for guests to note any allergies or dietary restrictions. This thoughtful touch ensures that everyone can fully enjoy the culinary delights you've prepared.

Keep Track: Create a system to keep track of RSVPs efficiently. Whether it's a spreadsheet, a dedicated RSVP platform, or even old-fashioned pen and paper, having a clear record of responses helps you stay organized and ensures that no detail is overlooked.

Follow-Up Communications: As the RSVP deadline approaches, send follow-up communications to those who haven't responded. Use this opportunity to express your eagerness to include them and address any potential obstacles they might be facing in making a decision.

Be Prepared for Surprises: Even with meticulous planning, expect some surprises. There might be last-minute RSVPs or unexpected changes. Embrace flexibility and be prepared to accommodate these surprises with grace, ensuring that your dinner party remains a joyful and stress-free affair.

Final Confirmation: In the days leading up to the event, send a final confirmation to all guests. This email can include essential details like the venue address, parking instructions, and any additional information to ensure a seamless experience for everyone.

Managing RSVPs is not just about gathering responses; it's about creating a positive and inclusive experience for your guests. By providing clear options, embracing technology, and maintaining open communication, you set the stage for a harmonious journey from invitation to celebration. So, as the responses roll in, celebrate each affirmative reply and graciously navigate any regrets. The art of RSVP management is an essential part of hosting, ensuring that your dinner party is not only well-attended but also filled with the energy and enthusiasm of those eagerly awaiting the delightful experience you've prepared for them. Get ready to welcome your guests with open arms as the RSVPs come in, and the countdown to your extraordinary dinner party begins!

Navigating Dinner Party Etiquette

As your dinner party approaches, it's time to delve into the finer points of dinner party etiquette, ensuring that the atmosphere is not only delicious but also characterized by warmth, consideration, and graciousness. In this section, we'll navigate through the nuances of etiquette, from welcoming your guests to bidding them farewell, ensuring that your gathering is not only a feast for the palate but also a celebration of thoughtful hospitality.

The Warm Welcome: As guests arrive, extend a warm and genuine welcome. Be at the door or designate someone to greet them, offering a friendly smile and a brief acknowledgment. A warm welcome sets a positive tone for the evening and makes guests feel valued and appreciated.

Introductions with Flair: If your guest list includes individuals who may not know each other, take the initiative to make introductions. A well-timed introduction can break the ice and create a comfortable atmosphere. Highlight common interests or connections to facilitate easy conversations.

Seating Gracefully: If your dinner involves assigned seating, guide guests to their designated seats with grace. A well-thought-out seating arrangement ensures a harmonious flow of conversation and connection. If it's an open seating arrangement, provide guidance on finding a seat without any rush or awkwardness.

The Art of Conversation: Encourage lively and inclusive conversations throughout the evening. As the host, take the lead in engaging with all guests, ensuring that no one feels left out. Be mindful of dominating discussions and make an effort to include everyone in the conversation.

Dietary Considerations: Be attentive to dietary considerations and restrictions. If your guests provided this information during the RSVP process, make an effort to accommodate their needs. If you're unsure, consider including a variety of options in your menu to cater to different preferences.

Toasting Etiquette: If you plan on making toasts during the dinner, be mindful of toasting etiquette. Keep toasts brief, avoid inside jokes that may exclude some guests, and raise your glass at the end to signal the toast. Encourage others to share their toasts, creating a celebratory atmosphere.

Pace of the Meal: Coordinate the pace of the meal to ensure a relaxed and enjoyable experience. Avoid rushing through courses, allowing guests to savor each dish and engage in unhurried conversation. Pay attention to the rhythm of the evening, ensuring a comfortable flow from appetizers to dessert.

Gracious Hosting: A gracious host is attentive, considerate, and makes an effort to ensure the comfort of their guests. Be present and engaged, but also allow your guests space to enjoy the company of others. Anticipate needs, such as refilling drinks or offering additional servings, without being intrusive.

Handling Unexpected Situations: Despite meticulous planning, unexpected situations may arise. Whether it's a spilled drink, a dietary mishap, or any other unforeseen circumstance, handle these situations with poise and a sense of humor. Guests will appreciate your grace under unexpected pressure.

Bidding Farewell: As the evening comes to a close, bid farewell to your guests with the same warmth with which you welcomed them. Express gratitude for their presence, and if applicable, provide small tokens of appreciation, such as party favors. Ensure that everyone departs feeling cherished and with fond memories of the evening.

Follow-Up Gratitude: Send a follow-up message expressing your gratitude for their attendance. A simple thank-you note or email reaffirms your appreciation and leaves a lasting positive impression.

Reflect and Learn: After the event, take time to reflect on the evening. Consider what worked well and what could be improved. Use this insight to refine your hosting skills for future gatherings, ensuring each one is a unique and delightful experience.

Navigating dinner party etiquette is an art that transforms a meal into a memorable celebration of hospitality. By embracing warmth, consideration, and graciousness, you create an atmosphere where guests feel not only nourished but also cherished. So, as you prepare to host your dinner party, let etiquette be your guide, weaving an invisible thread of thoughtfulness that elevates the entire experience. Get ready to navigate the nuances of etiquette with flair, ensuring that your gathering is not just a dinner party but a testament to the art of gracious hosting!

Chapter 5: The Art of Conversation

Welcome to Chapter 5: The Art of Conversation, where we dive into the heart of any successful dinner party—the lively and enriching exchange of words that weaves the fabric of connection. In this chapter, we embark on a journey beyond the culinary delights, exploring the nuances of engaging conversations that elevate your gathering from a meal to a memorable experience. The art of conversation is the alchemy that transforms a dinner party into a shared journey of laughter, stories, and genuine connections. From cultivating an inclusive atmosphere to navigating various conversational styles, we'll navigate the landscape of dialogue with warmth, curiosity, and a touch of charm. So, as you prepare to host your dinner party, let this chapter be your guide to fostering conversations that linger in the hearts of your guests long after the last dish is cleared. Get ready to master the art of conversation, making your gathering not just a feast for the senses but a celebration of the shared human experience.

Icebreakers and Conversation Starters

In the symphony of a dinner party, the initial notes set the tone for a harmonious evening. Enter the world of icebreakers and conversation starters –

the lively spark that ignites connections and transforms a room of individuals into a gathering of friends. In this section, we'll explore the art of breaking down barriers and initiating conversations that flow with ease and genuine warmth.

The Welcoming Icebreaker: As guests arrive, greet them with an icebreaker that eases them into the social rhythm of the evening. Simple yet effective, questions like "What's your favorite comfort food?" or "Share a memorable travel experience" open the door to personal narratives and set a positive tone for the conversations to come.

Themed Conversation Starters: Align conversation starters with the theme of your dinner party. If you're hosting a cultural feast, ask guests about their favorite international destinations or experiences. For a holiday celebration, delve into cherished traditions. Themed conversation starters not only tie into the overall ambiance but also provide a natural segue into the evening's festivities.

The Two-Truths-and-a-Lie Twist: Add an element of intrigue with a classic game of "Two Truths and a Lie." Each guest shares three statements about themselves – two true and one false. Others then guess which statement is the lie. This not only sparks laughter and curiosity but also reveals surprising aspects of each guest's personality.

Table Topics Cards: Consider incorporating Table Topics cards into your dinner party. These cards feature thought-provoking questions and conversation prompts that guests can draw from a deck. From light-hearted queries to more profound reflections, Table Topics cards offer a structured yet spontaneous way to stimulate engaging conversations.

The Memory Lane Opener: Invite guests to stroll down memory lane by sharing a memorable moment from their past. Whether it's a childhood escapade, a career achievement, or a funny anecdote, this icebreaker not only fosters connection but also provides insight into each guest's life story.

Personalized Place Cards: If your dinner involves assigned seating, consider adding a personalized touch to place cards. Include a fun fact or an interesting question related to each guest. This not only serves as an icebreaker but also sparks curiosity and creates an immediate point of connection.

Share a Hobby or Passion: Encourage guests to share their hobbies or passions. Whether it's gardening, photography, or a unique skill, discussing personal interests opens up avenues for engaging conversations. It's a wonderful way to discover shared enthusiasms and foster a sense of camaraderie.

The Culinary Conversation Starter: Given the backdrop of a dinner party, leverage the culinary setting to spark conversations. Ask guests about their favorite cuisines, memorable dining experiences, or even kitchen adventures. Food is a universal language, and conversations around it often lead to delightful discoveries.

Compliment Connection: Initiate conversations with genuine compliments. Whether it's praising a guest's attire, acknowledging a recent accomplishment, or expressing admiration for a shared interest, compliments create a positive atmosphere and provide a natural segue into meaningful conversations.

The Future Aspirations Quest: Shift the focus from the past to the future by asking guests about their aspirations. This icebreaker encourages guests to share their dreams, goals, and what they're looking forward to. It's an optimistic and forward-looking conversation starter that adds a touch of inspiration to the evening.

Open-Ended Wonderings: Foster open-ended conversations by asking wonderous questions. Instead of yes-or-no inquiries, pose questions that invite thoughtful responses. For example, "If you could have dinner with anyone, living or deceased, who would it be and why?" These types of questions encourage deeper discussions and allow guests to express their thoughts and feelings.

In the art of conversation, icebreakers and starters act as the gentle catalysts that transform initial hesitations into shared laughter and connection. As you infuse your dinner party with these conversation sparks, remember that the goal is not just to break the ice but to create an environment where conversations flow naturally and everyone feels valued and engaged. So, prepare to launch your dinner party into a realm of vibrant dialogue and camaraderie, where the art of conversation becomes the heart of the celebration!

Facilitating Meaningful Discussions

Beyond the initial icebreakers lies the heart of any memorable dinner party—the art of facilitating meaningful discussions. In this section, we'll explore how to guide conversations from surface-level pleasantries to the depth of shared experiences, creating an atmosphere where genuine connections flourish and the joy of conversation becomes the centerpiece of your gathering.

Active Listening: The foundation of meaningful discussions is active listening. Encourage guests to share their thoughts, stories, and perspectives, and listen attentively. When people feel heard, they're more likely to open up and engage in deeper conversations.

Thoughtful Questioning: Craft thoughtful questions that invite reflection and introspection. Instead of asking about the weather, delve into topics that encourage guests to share their passions, values, and aspirations. Questions like "What book has had a profound impact on your life?" or "If you could choose a superpower, what would it be and why?" prompt more meaningful responses.

Shared Experiences: Find common ground by exploring shared experiences. Whether it's a shared hobby, a common hometown, or similar career paths, shared experiences provide a foundation for connection. Foster discussions around these shared elements to deepen the sense of camaraderie.

Storytelling Magic: Encourage storytelling as a powerful means of connection. Invite guests to share personal anecdotes, funny incidents, or heartwarming memories. Storytelling not only creates a bond among guests but also adds a touch of warmth and authenticity to the conversation.

Vulnerability and Authenticity: Create a safe space for vulnerability and authenticity. Encourage guests to share not only their successes but also their challenges and aspirations. When conversations embrace authenticity, a deeper connection emerges, and guests feel more comfortable expressing their true selves.

Diverse Perspectives: Celebrate diversity in perspectives. A meaningful conversation thrives on the richness of different viewpoints. Encourage guests to share their unique experiences and opinions, fostering an atmosphere of respect and openness.

Guiding the Flow: As the host, gently guide the flow of conversations. Introduce new topics, bridge gaps between different conversations, and ensure that everyone has an opportunity to contribute. The art of guiding without dominating allows the organic flow of meaningful discussions.

Mindful Group Dynamics: Be mindful of group dynamics. If you notice someone less involved in the conversation, find ways to include them. Consider shifting the seating arrangement or introducing topics that align with their interests. Creating an inclusive atmosphere ensures that everyone feels valued and heard.

Reflection and Gratitude: Incorporate moments of reflection and gratitude into the conversation. Ask guests to share something they're grateful for or a lesson they've learned recently. These moments add a positive dimension to the discussions and create a shared appreciation for life's blessings.

Humor as a Bonding Element: Infuse humor into the conversation as a bonding element. Shared laughter creates a lighthearted atmosphere and strengthens the sense of connection among guests. Encourage guests to share funny stories or reminisce about amusing experiences.

Purposeful Transitions: Navigate purposeful transitions between topics. As discussions naturally evolve, guide the transition to new subjects to keep the conversation dynamic and engaging. Smooth transitions ensure a continuous flow of meaningful discussions.

Expressing Gratitude: Express gratitude for the shared moments and conversations. A simple acknowledgment of the enriching discussions adds a closing note of warmth and appreciation to the evening.

Facilitating meaningful discussions is an art that requires a delicate balance of active listening, thoughtful questioning, and creating an environment where authenticity flourishes. As you guide your guests through conversations that transcend the ordinary, remember that the true magic lies in fostering connections that linger long after the dinner plates have been cleared. So, as you embark on the journey of meaningful discussions, let the art of conversation become a celebration of shared experiences, laughter, and the joy of genuine connection!

Games and Activities

Elevate the energy and laughter at your dinner party by incorporating games and activities that infuse a playful spirit into the atmosphere. In this section, we'll explore creative ways to turn your gathering into an interactive and entertaining experience, ensuring that the art of conversation mingles seamlessly with the joy of shared activities.

Board Games and Trivia: Bring out classic board games or trivia sets that encourage friendly competition and collaboration. Games like Pictionary, Scrabble, or trivia relevant to your guests' interests add a fun and engaging element to the evening. These games provide a structured yet entertaining platform for guests to interact.

Conversation Card Decks: Introduce conversation card decks that feature thought-provoking questions and prompts. These decks, designed specifically for fostering meaningful discussions, can be passed around the table or placed strategically to ignite interesting conversations. It's a playful way to explore deeper topics and create connections.

Collaborative Cooking: Transform cooking into a collaborative and interactive experience. Set up a DIY pizza station, a make-your-own taco bar, or a dessert decorating corner. Not only does this engage guests in a shared activity, but it also adds a touch of culinary creativity to your dinner party.

Team Building Challenges: Organize team-building challenges that encourage collaboration. From building the tallest tower with everyday items to solving riddles together, these challenges create a lighthearted atmosphere and provide opportunities for guests to work together towards a common goal.

Memory Lane Photo Share: Invite guests to bring a meaningful photo or memento and share the story behind it. This activity not only sparks interesting conversations but also allows guests to connect on a personal level. It's a nostalgic journey that adds a sentimental touch to the evening.

Murder Mystery Dinners: Inject an element of mystery into your dinner party with a murder mystery game. Guests take on roles, and together, they work to unravel the mystery throughout the evening. It's an immersive and entertaining activity that fosters collaboration and adds a layer of intrigue to your gathering.

Table Games for Conversation: Incorporate table games specifically designed for fostering conversation. Games like "Would You Rather?" or "Two Truths and a Lie" can be adapted into a seated format, encouraging guests to share interesting facts or engage in amusing hypothetical scenarios.

Interactive Quizzes: Create interactive quizzes related to the theme of your dinner party. Whether it's a pop culture quiz, a culinary challenge, or a personalized trivia game about your guests, quizzes add an element of surprise and friendly competition to the gathering.

Karaoke Night: Turn your dinner party into a karaoke night. Provide a selection of songs that cater to different tastes and encourage guests to showcase their vocal talents. Karaoke adds a lively and entertaining dimension to the evening, creating memorable moments of laughter and camaraderie.

Artistic Expression Corner: Set up an artistic expression corner with materials for drawing or crafting. This activity allows guests to unleash their creativity and provides a casual space for conversations to flow naturally. The resulting artwork can serve as a unique memento from the evening.

Storytelling Circle: Create a storytelling circle where each guest contributes to a collaborative story. One person begins the tale, and others add to it as the circle continues. This interactive storytelling activity not only sparks creativity but also showcases the diverse imaginations of your guests.

Scavenger Hunt: If your dinner party involves different areas or rooms, organize a scavenger hunt. Create a list of items or clues related to the theme, and let guests explore and discover hidden treasures. It's a dynamic and engaging activity that adds an element of adventure to the evening.

Games and activities are the secret ingredients that infuse a sense of playfulness and camaraderie into your dinner party. As you incorporate these interactive elements, remember that the goal is to create an environment where laughter and connection flow effortlessly. So, whether it's a friendly competition, a collaborative challenge, or a creative endeavor, let games and activities become the catalysts that enhance the joy of shared moments and transform your dinner party into an unforgettable celebration!

Chapter 6: Troubleshooting and Quick Fixes

Welcome to Chapter 6: Troubleshooting and Quick Fixes, your go-to guide for navigating the unpredictable seas of hosting a dinner party. As we embark on this chapter, we acknowledge that even the most meticulously planned events can encounter unexpected hiccups. Fear not, for this chapter is your companion in turning challenges into opportunities and transforming potential pitfalls into moments of grace. From culinary conundrums to unforeseen logistics, we'll explore practical solutions and quick fixes that keep the spirit of your gathering alive and thriving. Think of it as your emergency kit for hosting—a collection of tips and tricks that will help you handle any unexpected twists with poise and a touch of humor.

So, whether it's a last-minute guest change, a kitchen mishap, or a sudden shift in weather, let this chapter be your reassuring guide. Together, we'll navigate the realm of troubleshooting, turning challenges into anecdotes and ensuring that the show, or in this case, the dinner party, must go on! Get ready to face the unexpected with confidence, knowing that every glitch is an opportunity to showcase your resilience and turn your dinner party into an adventure filled with laughter, camaraderie, and, of course, delicious surprises.

Managing Unexpected Issues

Even the most meticulously planned dinner parties can encounter unexpected issues that require a dash of quick thinking and a sprinkle of grace. In this section, we'll explore common challenges and equip you with practical solutions to navigate the unexpected twists and turns that may arise, ensuring that your dinner party sails smoothly through any storm.

Last-Minute Guest Changes

Scenario: You receive a call an hour before the party—your friend's plus-one can't make it.

Quick Fix: Embrace flexibility and adjust the seating arrangement if necessary. Consider rearranging place cards or adapting the table setting to accommodate the change. A warm welcome awaits the revised guest list, ensuring everyone feels valued and included.

Kitchen Mishaps

Scenario: The main course is nearly ready, and you realize a key ingredient is missing.

Quick Fix: Improvise! A quick online search might offer substitutes. If that fails, don your apron, and get creative with the ingredients at hand. Flexibility and a sense of adventure can turn a potential kitchen crisis into a culinary triumph.

Weather Woes

Scenario: An unexpected rain shower threatens your outdoor dinner setup.

Quick Fix: Have a backup plan in mind. If possible, move the party indoors or set up a covered area. Alternatively, provide umbrellas or rain ponchos for an alfresco dining experience with a touch of adventure.

Technological Troubles

Scenario: Your carefully curated playlist suddenly refuses to cooperate.

Quick Fix: Keep a backup playlist or switch to a music streaming service with ready-made playlists. Alternatively, encourage guests to share their favorite songs, turning a technical glitch into a collaborative and personalized musical experience.

Unforeseen Dietary Restrictions

Scenario: A guest reveals a dietary restriction that wasn't communicated during the RSVP.

Quick Fix: Stay calm and assess the menu. With a well-stocked kitchen, you can often whip up an alternative dish. If not, consider modifying a part of the menu to accommodate the dietary restriction. Apologize graciously, and assure the guest that their comfort is a priority.

Power Outage

Scenario: The lights flicker, and suddenly you find yourself in darkness.

Quick Fix: Keep candles or battery-operated lanterns on hand for an instant, cozy ambiance. If your cooking relies on electricity, a gas grill or stovetop can save the day. Transform the unexpected power outage into an intimate, candlelit dinner experience.

Seating Dilemmas

Scenario: Two guests seem to clash, and you sense tension at the table.

Quick Fix: Shuffle the seating arrangement subtly. Introduce conversation topics that bridge diverse interests or create a diversion that shifts the focus. The goal is to maintain a harmonious atmosphere without drawing attention to any underlying tensions.

Time Crunch

Scenario: The clock is ticking, and you're running behind schedule.

Quick Fix: Simplify. Focus on the essentials and delegate tasks if possible. Guests are more forgiving than you might think, and the key is to remain composed. A well-paced, enjoyable evening is more important than adhering strictly to a timetable.

Communication Hiccups

Scenario: Miscommunication leads to a misunderstanding about the start time.

Quick Fix: Apologize sincerely and gracefully adjust. Offer a small appetizer or aperitif while guests arrive, turning the situation into an opportunity for an extended welcome and relaxed start to the evening.

Navigating unexpected issues with a calm and adaptable mindset is the hallmark of a seasoned host. As you encounter these twists, remember that the true essence of a dinner party lies in the shared experience and connections forged, rather than the flawless execution of plans. So, face the unexpected with a smile, and let each hiccup become a memorable part of your dinner party narrative—a tale to be told with humor and camaraderie in the days to come. Get ready to transform challenges into triumphs and showcase your hosting resilience with flair!

Quick Fixes for Common Problems

In the bustling world of hosting, a few quick fixes can turn potential disasters into minor hiccups. In this section, we'll explore common problems that may arise during your dinner party and provide simple, effective solutions to keep the celebration on track. These quick fixes are your secret weapons, ready to be deployed with a smile and a sprinkle of ingenuity.

Emergency Seating

Problem: Unexpected extra guests and not enough seats.

Quick Fix: Create a cozy lounge area with cushions or repurpose sturdy ottomans as additional seating. For a casual affair, a picnic-style setup with blankets on the floor can add a touch of charm while accommodating more guests than anticipated.

Wine Stains

Problem: A guest accidentally spills red wine on the tablecloth or their clothing.

Quick Fix: For tablecloths, act quickly by blotting the stain with a clean cloth and sprinkling salt to absorb the wine. For clothing, dab the stain with a mixture of white wine and salt or use club soda. In both cases, avoid rubbing to prevent the stain from setting.

Cold Food, Warm Guests

Problem: The meal is ready, but guests are not at the table yet.

Quick Fix: Keep dishes warm in the oven on low heat or use chafing dishes. For individual plates, warm them in the oven briefly before serving. Covering dishes with foil helps retain heat, ensuring your guests enjoy a delicious, hot meal.

Uneven Conversations

Problem: One guest feels left out of the conversation.

Quick Fix: Act as the bridge. Gently guide the conversation to include everyone, or introduce a topic that aligns with the guest's interests. Thoughtful seating arrangements can also prevent isolated moments, ensuring a harmonious flow of conversation.

Forgot an Ingredient

Problem: A crucial ingredient is missing from your recipe.

Quick Fix: Improvise! Search your pantry for substitutes or get creative with what you have on hand. Many dishes can tolerate minor adjustments, turning a missing ingredient into an opportunity for culinary experimentation.

Limited Drink Options

Problem: Running out of a popular drink option.

Quick Fix: Introduce a signature mocktail or spritzer using available ingredients. This not only provides an alternative but also adds a personalized touch to your beverage offerings. For alcoholic options, a DIY cocktail station can keep the spirits flowing.

Dessert Disaster
Problem: The dessert doesn't turn out as expected.

Quick Fix: Transform it into a deconstructed dessert or create a dessert platter with a variety of options. Garnish creatively to enhance the presentation. Dessert mishaps can become an unexpected highlight with a touch of improvisation.

In the world of hosting, quick fixes are your allies, ready to transform challenges into opportunities and keep the energy of your dinner party vibrant. Remember, the essence of hosting lies in creating an atmosphere of warmth and connection, and these quick fixes are the tools that help you navigate any bumps along the way with style and grace. So, embrace the unexpected, keep your quick fixes close at hand, and let each challenge become a story to share and laugh about in the future. Get ready to host with confidence, knowing that your quick fixes are the magic touch that turns every hiccup into a moment of hosting brilliance!

Maintaining Your Composure

Hosting a dinner party is a joyful endeavor, but unexpected challenges can test even the most seasoned hosts. In this section, we'll explore the art of maintaining your composure when faced with unforeseen hiccups. These tips will not only help you navigate challenges gracefully but also ensure that the spirit of your dinner party remains vibrant and positive.

Embrace Imperfections: Perfection is an elusive goal, especially in the dynamic world of hosting. Embrace the imperfections, understanding that they often add character and create memorable stories. Your guests are there to enjoy the experience, not to scrutinize every detail. A calm and collected host sets the tone for an enjoyable evening.

Breathe and Prioritize: When faced with multiple challenges, take a moment to breathe and prioritize. Identify the most critical issues that need immediate attention and address them calmly. Accept that not everything will go according to plan, and that's perfectly okay. By focusing on what truly matters, you can maintain a sense of control and composure.

Delegate with Confidence: You don't have to handle everything on your own. Delegate tasks confidently, whether it's enlisting a friend to assist in the kitchen or asking a guest for help with a specific aspect of the party. Delegating not only eases your workload but also fosters a sense of collaboration among your guests.

Keep Smiling: A genuine smile is your secret weapon. Even in the face of challenges, maintaining a positive and cheerful demeanor helps diffuse tension and reassure your guests. A smile communicates that you're enjoying the moment, and your guests will likely follow suit.

Laugh at the Mishaps: Laughter is a powerful tool for diffusing stress. When a mishap occurs, find the humor in the situation and share a laugh with your guests. Whether it's a kitchen escapade or a unexpected turn of events, approaching it with a lighthearted attitude can turn a potential stressor into a bonding moment.

Roll with the Punches: In the unpredictable world of hosting, the ability to adapt is crucial. Roll with the punches and be flexible in your approach. If the weather shifts unexpectedly or a dish doesn't turn out as planned, consider it an opportunity to showcase your resilience and ability to navigate the unexpected.

Focus on Guest Experience: Shift your focus from the challenges to the guest experience. Guests are unlikely to notice minor glitches if they are immersed in a positive and enjoyable atmosphere. By prioritizing the well-being and enjoyment of your guests, you redirect attention away from any behind-the-scenes challenges.

Learn to Let Go: Some things are beyond your control, and that's perfectly fine. Learn to let go of perfectionistic tendencies and embrace the ebb and flow of hosting. Your guests are there to share good times, and your composure in the face of challenges contributes to the overall positive energy of the gathering.

Take Breaks Strategically: If you find yourself feeling overwhelmed, strategically take short breaks. Stepping away for a moment allows you to regroup and refocus. Whether it's a brief moment in another room or a step outside for fresh air, these breaks can be rejuvenating and help you maintain your composure.

Reflect Post-Party: After the event, take time to reflect on the evening. Acknowledge what went well, appreciate the moments of joy, and consider any challenges as opportunities for growth. By adopting a reflective mindset, you gain insights that can enhance your hosting skills for future gatherings.

Maintaining your composure as a host is an art that evolves with practice. By embracing the unexpected, focusing on the positive, and navigating challenges with grace, you not only ensure a memorable experience for your guests but also cultivate a sense of confidence and joy in your role as a host. So, as you embark on your hosting journey, remember that maintaining your composure is the key to transforming any hiccup into a triumph and ensuring that your dinner party is a celebration of warmth, connection, and shared moments!

Chapter 7: Creating Lasting Memories

Welcome to Chapter 7: Creating Lasting Memories, the heartwarming culmination of your journey in hosting a dinner party. As we venture into this chapter, we shift our focus from the logistics and challenges to the essence of hosting—an unforgettable experience that lingers in the hearts and minds of your guests. Here, we explore the art of crafting moments that transcend the ordinary, turning your dinner party into a tapestry of memories that will be cherished for years to come.

In these pages, we delve into the subtle alchemy of ambiance, the magic of meaningful conversations, and the power of shared activities that leave a lasting imprint. Creating memories is an art that goes beyond the menu and décor; it's about curating an atmosphere where laughter, connection, and joy become the legacy of your gathering.

From capturing candid photographs to weaving personalized touches into your hosting style, this chapter guides you in transforming your dinner party into a treasure trove of memories. As you navigate the various elements that contribute to a memorable evening, remember that the true beauty lies in the genuine moments shared—the hearty laughter around the table, the stories exchanged, and the warmth that lingers in the air.

So, let this chapter be your companion in the final steps of your hosting journey. Whether you're hosting an intimate gathering or a grand celebration, the principles shared here are timeless, adaptable to any occasion. Get ready to infuse your dinner party with the magic that turns fleeting hours into cherished memories, making your hosting venture not just an event but a legacy of connection, laughter, and the enduring joy of shared moments.

Capturing the Moment

In the kaleidoscope of a memorable dinner party, one of the keys to preserving the magic is capturing the moment. As we explore this section, we'll dive into the art of photography, the nuances of candid shots, and the subtle ways to document the laughter, connection, and joy that define your gathering. After all, the images we create become the visual narrative of the evening, weaving together a tapestry of memories that will be revisited and cherished for years to come.

Candid Moments: The beauty of a candid photograph lies in its authenticity. Encourage your guests to be themselves, capturing the unscripted laughter, animated conversations, and the spontaneous joy that unfolds naturally. Candid shots provide a genuine glimpse into the heart of your dinner party, reflecting the warmth and camaraderie that make the event special.

Thoughtful Settings: Set the stage for memorable photos with thoughtful and well-curated settings. Consider the lighting, backdrop, and overall ambiance when selecting areas for group photos or individual portraits. A well-chosen setting enhances the visual appeal of your photos and adds an extra layer of charm to the memories captured.

Guest Photo Contributions: Invite your guests to contribute their photos from the evening. Whether through a shared album on a digital platform or a designated hashtag for social media, incorporating guest-contributed photos adds diverse perspectives and captures moments you may have missed. It transforms the documentation of the evening into a collaborative effort, fostering a sense of shared memories.

Personalized Touches: Infuse personalized touches into your photo documentation. Create a DIY photo booth with props that align with the theme of your party, encouraging guests to take playful and creative photos. Alternatively, provide disposable cameras on tables, allowing guests to capture candid moments from their unique viewpoints.

Unplugged Intervals: Consider designating certain intervals of the evening as "unplugged" moments. During these times, encourage guests to put away their devices and immerse themselves fully in the present. Whether it's during toasts, games, or a particularly special part of the evening, these unplugged intervals create authentic moments free from screens and distractions.

Group Dynamics: Capture the dynamics of your guest group. Take a mix of full-group photos and smaller, more intimate shots. Group photos provide a snapshot of the collective energy, while smaller shots capture the depth of individual connections. A variety of groupings ensures a diverse representation of the evening's atmosphere.

Storytelling through Photos: Craft a visual storytelling experience with your photos. Arrange them in a chronological order or create themed albums that showcase different aspects of the evening. As you curate the images, think about the narrative you want to convey—the progression from arrival to lively conversations to the heartfelt farewells.

Spontaneity in Poses: Encourage spontaneity in posing for photos. Instead of rigid poses, let guests express themselves naturally. Capture the impromptu dance moves, the shared glances, and the genuine expressions that define the essence of the moment.

Spontaneous poses radiate authenticity and contribute to the narrative of the evening.

Expressive Details: Zoom in on expressive details—the clinking of glasses, the shared glances, the intricate table settings. These close-up shots add a layer of intimacy to your visual narrative, highlighting the intricate details that contribute to the overall ambiance of your dinner party.

Professional Touch: Consider hiring a photographer for significant events or milestones. A professional photographer brings a unique skill set to capture the essence of the evening with an artistic eye. Their expertise in framing shots, managing lighting, and documenting key moments can elevate the quality of your visual memories.

As you embark on the journey of capturing the moment, remember that each photograph is a brushstroke in the canvas of your dinner party memories. Whether through candid shots, group photos, or personalized touches, the art of capturing the moment allows you to preserve the magic and create a visual legacy of the joy, connection, and shared moments that define your hosting venture. So, pick up that camera or smartphone, let the creativity flow, and embark on the delightful task of preserving the memories that will be cherished for years to come!

Follow-Up and Thank Yous

The echoes of your dinner party may linger in the air, but the journey isn't complete without a thoughtful follow-up. This section explores the art of extending gratitude, sharing memories, and nurturing the connections forged during your gathering. As we delve into this section, let's uncover the joy of expressing appreciation and weaving the final threads that bind your dinner party into a tapestry of lasting memories.

Expressing Gratitude: In the days following your dinner party, express your gratitude to your guests for sharing in the celebration. A heartfelt thank-you message, whether through a handwritten note, an email, or a personalized text, conveys your appreciation for their presence, contributions, and the warmth they added to the evening.

Memory Lane: Revisit the memories collectively created by sharing a recap of the evening. This could take the form of a digital album with selected photos, a short video montage, or even a social media post that highlights the key moments. By curating and sharing these memories, you extend the joy of the event beyond the night itself.

Highlight Individual Contributions: Acknowledge and highlight the unique contributions of your guests. Whether someone brought a homemade dish, shared a memorable story, or contributed in a special way, recognizing these individual efforts shows that their presence was valued and their contributions made a meaningful impact on the overall experience.

Recipe Sharing: If your dinner party involved a culinary adventure, consider sharing the recipes from the evening. Compile a digital or physical recipe booklet with contributions from each dish. Not only does this serve as a delightful keepsake, but it also allows guests to recreate the magic of the evening in their own homes.

Personalized Thank-You Cards: Elevate your gratitude with personalized thank-you cards. Include a brief note expressing your appreciation, recounting a shared moment, or referencing a specific contribution from each guest. The personal touch of a handwritten note adds a thoughtful and lasting impression.

Virtual Toast: Organize a virtual toast as a post-party gathering. Whether through a video call or a virtual platform, a collective toast provides an opportunity to reconnect, share additional stories, and collectively reminisce about the highlights of the evening. It's a virtual extension of the warmth experienced during the party.

Future Gatherings: Plant the seeds for future gatherings. Mention your intention to host more events or express excitement about attending future get-togethers hosted by your guests. This not only maintains the momentum of connection but also fosters a sense of anticipation for the next shared experience.

Reflect on Feedback: Reflect on any feedback received from your guests. Whether it's a compliment on the menu, a mention of a particularly enjoyable activity, or suggestions for future gatherings, this feedback provides valuable insights. Use it to refine your hosting skills and enhance the experience for future events.

Social Media Sharing: Share moments from your dinner party on social media, if appropriate. Use platforms like Instagram or Facebook to showcase selected photos, express gratitude, and tag guests in your posts. It's a modern way to extend the celebration and create a digital footprint of the memories created.

Hand-Delivered Tokens: Consider hand-delivering small tokens of appreciation to your guests. This could be a potted plant, a small dessert, or a personalized trinket that serves as a physical reminder of the evening. The act of hand-delivering adds a personal touch and allows for a brief, post-party connection.

In the art of follow-up and thank-yous, the goal is to extend the joy of the dinner party beyond the confines of the event itself. Whether through heartfelt notes, shared memories, or expressions of anticipation for future gatherings, this final chapter completes the hosting journey, leaving a legacy of warmth, connection, and enduring memories. So, with gratitude in your heart and memories in your hands, embark on this final stage of your hosting adventure, ensuring that the spirit of your dinner party lives on in the hearts of your guests and in the collective memory you've created together.

Building a Tradition

As the curtain falls on your recent dinner party, the opportunity arises to transform a singular event into a cherished tradition. This section is an exploration of the art of building a tradition—an enduring thread that weaves through time, connecting past gatherings with the promise of future celebrations. In this section, we'll delve into the elements that contribute to the formation of traditions, turning your dinner party into a perennial source of joy, connection, and shared memories.

Reflect on the Essence: Begin by reflecting on the essence of your dinner party. What made it unique? Was it the menu, the ambiance, the activities, or the people? Identify the elements that contributed most to the warmth and enjoyment of the evening, as these will be the pillars on which your tradition stands.

Choose a Signature Element: Select a signature element that will become the cornerstone of your tradition. It could be a special dish, a themed decoration, a particular activity, or even a unique way of expressing gratitude. This signature element serves as the anchor, creating a sense of continuity from one celebration to the next.

Establish a Regular Cadence: Building a tradition involves regularity. Determine a cadence for your gatherings, whether it's a monthly, quarterly, or annual event. Consistency fosters anticipation and allows the tradition to take root, becoming an integral part of the social calendar for both you and your guests.

Involve Your Guests: Make your guests active participants in the tradition-building process. Seek their input on elements they enjoyed and aspects they would like to see continued. Involving your guests ensures that the tradition is a collective endeavor, creating a sense of ownership and shared responsibility.

Evolve and Adapt: Traditions are not static; they evolve over time. Be open to adaptation and refinement based on the changing dynamics of your social circle, the preferences of your guests, and the evolving context of your gatherings. A tradition that can flex and adapt is one that stands the test of time.

Document and Share Memories: Document each iteration of your dinner party tradition. Capture photographs, jot down anecdotes, and create a scrapbook or digital album that chronicles the evolution of the tradition. Sharing these memories with your guests adds depth to the tradition and creates a narrative that extends beyond individual events.

Introduce Rituals: Incorporate meaningful rituals into your tradition. These could be as simple as a toast to friendship, a shared moment of reflection, or a specific activity that marks the beginning or end of each gathering. Rituals add a layer of symbolism and continuity, anchoring the tradition in shared experiences.

Encourage Guest Contributions: Encourage your guests to contribute to the tradition. Whether it's through bringing a dish, suggesting an activity, or sharing their own traditions, guest contributions enrich the fabric of the tradition and create a sense of collaboration and shared ownership.

Plan for Milestones: Consider incorporating milestone celebrations into your tradition. Whether it's an anniversary of the first dinner party, a special theme for a significant gathering, or a surprise element to mark a milestone, these intentional moments add depth and significance to the tradition.

Pass it On: As your dinner party tradition takes root, consider passing it on to others. Invite friends or family to host their own version of the tradition, fostering a network of interconnected celebrations. The act of passing on the tradition ensures its continuity and introduces it to new circles of people.

Building a tradition is a journey of intention, connection, and shared joy. As you embark on this path, remember that traditions are not just about the events themselves but about the enduring connections they foster. Whether it's an annual feast, a monthly gathering, or a quarterly celebration, the tradition you build becomes a thread that weaves through the fabric of your social landscape, creating a tapestry of memories that enrich the lives of all who participate. So, with a heart full of anticipation and a spirit of continuity, embrace the art of building a tradition—one that promises to be a perennial source of joy, connection, and cherished memories for years to come.

Chapter 8: Beyond the Basics: Themes and Special Occasions

Welcome to Chapter 8: Beyond the Basics, where we embark on a delightful exploration of themes and special occasions that elevate your dinner parties to extraordinary experiences. This chapter is your passport to a world of creative possibilities, offering inspiration and guidance on how to infuse unique themes, celebrate special occasions, and turn your gatherings into memorable events that linger in the hearts and minds of your guests.

In these pages, we'll delve into the art of theme selection, uncovering ways to transform your dining space into a captivating setting that aligns with your chosen concept. From seasonal celebrations to whimsical themes that add a touch of playfulness, this chapter provides a palette of ideas to suit various tastes and occasions.

Whether you're hosting a cozy gathering for friends or planning a grand celebration for a milestone, the themes and special occasions explored in this chapter will spark your creativity and guide you in curating an immersive experience. Discover how to tailor your menu, décor, and activities to suit the chosen theme, creating a cohesive and enchanting atmosphere that leaves a lasting impression.

So, let your imagination take flight as we venture beyond the basics, exploring the realm of themes and special occasions. Whether you're drawn to elegant soirées, casual backyard barbecues, or whimsical celebrations, this chapter is your companion in crafting unforgettable moments. Get ready to infuse your dinner parties with a dash of magic and a sprinkle of uniqueness, making each gathering a celebration that goes beyond the ordinary and becomes a cherished chapter in your hosting journey.

Themed Dinner Parties

Immersing your guests in a carefully curated theme transforms a regular dinner party into an extraordinary experience. We'll explore the art of themed dinner parties—a delightful journey that goes beyond the ordinary, infusing your gathering with creativity, style, and a touch of magic. Let's dive into the world of themed dinner parties, where the menu, décor, and activities harmonize to create a cohesive and captivating atmosphere.

Choosing the Perfect Theme: The first step in hosting a themed dinner party is choosing the perfect theme. Whether it's a cultural celebration, a seasonal festivity, or a whimsical concept inspired by your favorite movie or book, the theme sets the stage for the entire event. Consider the preferences of your guests, the occasion, and the overall atmosphere you want to create.

Crafting a Theme-Infused Menu: Once you've selected a theme, the menu becomes an exciting canvas for culinary creativity. Tailor your dishes to complement the theme, incorporating flavors, ingredients, and presentation styles that align with the chosen concept. A themed menu not only tantalizes the taste buds but also enhances the overall immersive experience for your guests.

Atmosphere Through Décor: Transform your dining space into a visual feast that reflects the chosen theme. From table settings and centerpieces to lighting and color schemes, every element contributes to creating the desired atmosphere. For a tropical theme, vibrant colors and floral arrangements might take center stage, while a vintage Hollywood theme may call for elegant, black-and-white décor.

Dressing the Part: Encourage your guests to embrace the theme by dressing the part. Whether it's elegant attire for a formal affair or costumes for a whimsical theme, dressing in accordance with the concept adds an extra layer of fun and engagement. Provide suggestions or guidelines to help guests feel comfortable and excited about embracing the theme.

Interactive Theme Activities: Incorporate interactive activities that align with the theme to keep the energy high. For a 1920s Gatsby theme, consider a dance floor with jazz music, or for a beach luau, set up a DIY lei-making station. Interactive activities not only enhance the theme but also create memorable moments that elevate the overall experience.

Themed Music Playlists: Enhance the auditory dimension of your themed dinner party with curated playlists. Select music that complements the theme, setting the tone and immersing guests in the atmosphere you've created. From classical tunes for a formal affair to energetic beats for a festive theme, music adds a layer of sophistication to the experience.

Signature Theme Cocktails: Elevate your beverage offerings with signature theme cocktails. Create concoctions that reflect the flavors and colors associated with the chosen theme. Whether it's a fruity concoction for a tropical theme or a classic martini for a Hollywood glamour night, signature cocktails add a personalized touch to the evening.

Theme Reinforcements: Throughout the evening, reinforce the theme with subtle touches and surprises. Consider thematic favors or small tokens that guests can take home as mementos. Introduce unexpected elements that align with the theme, creating a sense of discovery and delight.

Photo Booth Extravaganza: Set up a themed photo booth to capture the joy and creativity of the evening. Provide props and backdrops that align with the theme, encouraging guests to strike poses and create memorable snapshots. The photo booth becomes a fun and interactive element that adds to the overall thematic experience.

Reflecting on the Theme: As the evening unfolds, take a moment to reflect on the success of the theme. Observe how guests embrace the concept, interact with the themed elements, and contribute to the overall atmosphere. This reflection not only provides insights for future themed events but also enhances your ability to create immersive and memorable experiences.

Themed dinner parties are a captivating way to infuse your gatherings with personality, creativity, and a sense of adventure. By thoughtfully incorporating the theme into every aspect of the event, you create a cohesive and enchanting atmosphere that resonates with your guests. So, whether you're planning an elegant masquerade, a rustic farmhouse feast, or a whimsical fairy-tale soirée, let the magic of themed dinner parties take your hosting journey to new heights, making each gathering a unique and unforgettable celebration.

Hosting for Special Occasions

Special occasions deserve celebrations that go beyond the ordinary, and hosting for these moments allows you to create unforgettable memories that linger for a lifetime. In this section, we explore the art of hosting for special occasions, from milestone birthdays to anniversaries, graduations, and everything in between. Let's dive into the joyous world of commemorating significant moments with thoughtfulness, creativity, and a touch of personalization.

Tailoring the Celebration: When hosting for a special occasion, the key is tailoring every aspect of the celebration to honor the significance of the moment. Consider the preferences, interests, and personality of the guest of honor or the occasion being celebrated. This thoughtful approach ensures that the celebration feels deeply personal and resonates with the spirit of the event.

Personalized Invitations: Set the tone for the special occasion with personalized invitations. Craft invitations that reflect the theme or mood of the celebration, incorporating elements that hint at the unique character of the event. Whether it's a formal printed invitation or a creative digital design, personalized invitations build anticipation and convey the importance of the occasion.

Signature Decor Elements: Elevate the ambiance with signature decor elements that symbolize the essence of the special occasion. This could be a customized centerpiece, thematic decorations, or even a visual timeline that reflects the journey leading up to the celebration. The goal is to create an atmosphere that feels tailor-made for the momentous occasion.

Meaningful Milestone Reflections: Take a moment during the celebration to reflect on the milestones and achievements being honored. This could involve a speech, a tribute video, or a symbolic gesture that acknowledges the journey leading up to the special occasion. Meaningful reflections deepen the emotional connection and enhance the overall significance of the celebration.

Thoughtful Gift-Giving: Gift-giving becomes a centerpiece of hosting for special occasions. Thoughtfully select gifts that align with the interests and preferences of the guest of honor or the occasion being celebrated. Consider personalized touches, such as custom engravings or sentimental items, to add an extra layer of thoughtfulness to the gift-giving experience.

Tailored Menu with Favorites: Craft a menu that features the favorite dishes and flavors of the guest of honor. Whether it's a selection of cherished family recipes or a menu inspired by their culinary preferences, tailoring the culinary experience adds a personal touch to the celebration. Consider incorporating favorite desserts, signature drinks, or nostalgic dishes.

Interactive Memory Sharing: Invite guests to share memories, anecdotes, or well-wishes during the celebration. This interactive element not only engages attendees but also creates a collective narrative that contributes to the overall joy and sentiment of the occasion. Provide a platform for guests to express their thoughts, whether through a guestbook, a memory jar, or a dedicated sharing session.

Incorporating Symbolic Elements: Incorporate symbolic elements that represent the essence of the special occasion. This could involve a ceremonial lighting, a symbolic gesture, or the inclusion of meaningful symbols that hold significance for the guest of honor or the theme of the celebration. Symbolic elements deepen the emotional resonance of the event.

Themed Entertainment: Enhance the celebratory atmosphere with themed entertainment. Whether it's a live band, a DJ playing favorite songs, or a performance that aligns with the theme of the occasion, entertainment adds a dynamic and festive element to the celebration. Consider incorporating elements that resonate with the guest of honor or the overall theme.

Creating a Keepsake: As a final touch, create a keepsake or memento that guests can take home to commemorate the special occasion. This could be a personalized favor, a commemorative photo, or a small item that serves as a tangible reminder of the celebration. Keepsakes become cherished tokens that extend the memory of the occasion beyond the event itself.

Hosting for special occasions is a heartfelt opportunity to celebrate the milestones, achievements, and joyous moments that shape our lives. By tailoring every aspect of the celebration to the significance of the occasion, you create an immersive and unforgettable experience that resonates with the hearts of your guests. So, whether you're raising a toast to an anniversary, marking a significant birthday, or commemorating a life achievement, let the art of hosting for special occasions be your guide in creating moments that are as unique and special as the celebrations they honor.

Elevating Your Skills - Advanced Hosting Techniques

As you journey deeper into the realm of hosting, this section invites you to elevate your skills with advanced hosting techniques. Beyond the basics and themes, these techniques are the secret ingredients that transform a gathering into an exquisite experience. In this section, we'll explore nuanced strategies, refined touches, and expert-level approaches that set the stage for hosting mastery.

Expert-Level Menu Planning: Take your menu planning to the next level by incorporating unexpected flavor pairings, intricate presentations, and culinary techniques that showcase your skills. Experiment with molecular gastronomy, create a themed tasting menu, or explore international fusion cuisine. An expert-level menu is a feast for the senses, leaving a lasting impression on your guests.

Sommelier-Style Beverage Pairing: Elevate your beverage offerings by mastering the art of pairing. Consider consulting with a sommelier or researching wine and cocktail pairings that complement each course of your menu. From wine flights to artisanal cocktails, thoughtful beverage pairings enhance the overall dining experience and demonstrate a sophisticated approach to hosting.

Personalized Guest Experiences: Craft personalized experiences for your guests that go beyond the ordinary. Consider individualized menus tailored to dietary preferences, custom welcome gifts, or even a dedicated concierge service for larger events. By anticipating and catering to the unique needs and preferences of your guests, you create a level of hospitality that is both memorable and unparalleled.

Artistic Tablescaping: Transform your table into a work of art with meticulous tablescaping. Explore creative tablecloth and napkin folds, experiment with elaborate centerpieces, and curate a visual narrative that aligns with the theme or ambiance you wish to convey. Artistic tablescaping adds a layer of sophistication to your hosting, immersing guests in a visually stunning dining environment.

Culinary Demonstrations and Workshops: Infuse interactive elements into your gatherings by incorporating culinary demonstrations or workshops. Whether it's a live cooking show, a cocktail mixing session, or a dessert-making workshop, involving guests in the culinary process adds an engaging and educational dimension to the event, creating a memorable experience.

Seamless Event Coordination: Master the art of event coordination to ensure seamless execution. Whether you're hosting an intimate dinner party or a grand celebration, meticulous planning and coordination are essential. Consider creating a detailed timeline, coordinating with vendors, and having contingency plans in place. A well-coordinated event allows you to focus on connecting with your guests, knowing that the logistics are expertly managed.

Advanced Theme Integration: Take your themed events to new heights with advanced theme integration. This involves a deeper exploration of thematic elements, incorporating symbolism, and infusing subtle details that enhance the overall narrative. Advanced theme integration creates a more immersive experience, transporting guests to a carefully crafted world that aligns with the chosen concept.

Thoughtful Seating Arrangements: Elevate your approach to seating arrangements by considering the dynamics and connections among your guests. Thoughtful placement enhances conversation flow, fosters connections, and ensures that each guest feels considered and valued. Experiment with different seating configurations to find the arrangement that best suits the atmosphere you want to create.

Incorporating Live Entertainment: Enhance the atmosphere with live entertainment that aligns with the mood and theme of your gathering. This could include live music, a professional DJ, or even specialty performers that add an element of surprise and delight. Live entertainment contributes to the overall ambiance, creating a dynamic and engaging experience for your guests.

Advanced Problem-Solving: Become adept at advanced problem-solving to navigate unexpected challenges with grace. Whether it's a last-minute change in guest count, a culinary mishap, or unforeseen logistical issues, the ability to problem-solve on the spot ensures that your event runs smoothly. Cultivate flexibility, resourcefulness, and a calm demeanor to handle any curveballs that may come your way.

Elevating your skills with advanced hosting techniques is a continuous journey of growth and refinement. By integrating expert-level approaches into your hosting repertoire, you create experiences that are not only memorable but also showcase your passion for hospitality. As you explore these advanced techniques, remember that the essence of hosting lies in the joy of connecting with others and creating moments that are as delightful as they are unforgettable. So, embark on this advanced hosting adventure with enthusiasm, creativity, and the confidence that comes from mastering the art of hospitality.

Conclusion: A Culinary Canvas of Connection

As we draw the final curtain on this journey through the art of hosting a dinner party, it's with a heart full of gratitude, a head brimming with memories, and the realization that hosting is not merely an event—it's a canvas for creating connections and crafting moments that linger in the hearts of all who partake. We've navigated the intricacies of setting the stage, planning menus, mastering tablescapes, and exploring the magic of themed and special occasion gatherings. Together, we've uncovered the nuances that transform a gathering into a celebration, a feast into a symphony, and a dinner party into an art form.

At the heart of hosting lies the simple yet profound act of bringing people together. Beyond the carefully selected menus and elegantly arranged tablescapes, beyond the themed décor and entertainment, hosting is about the alchemy that occurs when individuals gather around a shared table. It's about the stories exchanged, the laughter that resonates, and the connections forged over a delicious meal. It's the shared delight in a culinary creation, the clinking of glasses in celebration, and the warmth that emanates from a table where friendships are nourished and memories are cultivated.

Throughout this book, we've delved into the practicalities of hosting, offering tips, insights, and step-by-step guidance to help you orchestrate gatherings with finesse. Yet, beneath the surface of logistics and planning, the true essence of hosting lies in the intangible—the intangible magic that happens when you open your home, your kitchen, and your heart to others.

As you embark on your hosting adventures, remember that perfection is not the goal; rather, it's the authenticity of the experience that makes it truly special. Embrace the beauty of imperfection, the unexpected mishaps, and the delightful surprises that weave into the fabric of your gatherings. Hosting is an ever-evolving art, and each event is an opportunity to refine your skills, learn from the unexpected, and infuse your unique personality into the tapestry of hospitality you create.

Beyond the tangible elements of hosting, the intangibles are what make a gathering unforgettable. It's the way a well-placed candlelight casts a warm glow, the way a shared anecdote elicits laughter, and the way a thoughtful gesture lingers in the hearts of your guests. Hosting is about creating a space where people feel seen, heard, and valued—a space where connections deepen, and bonds strengthen.

As you continue your hosting journey, embrace the joy of experimentation and the thrill of discovery. Try new recipes, explore different themes, and infuse your gatherings with the creativity that reflects your unique style. Whether you're hosting an intimate dinner for close friends, a festive celebration for a special occasion, or a themed extravaganza that transports guests to another world, let your personality shine through, creating an experience that is distinctly yours.

In the grand tapestry of hosting, you are the artist, and each gathering is a stroke on the canvas of connection. So, with a heart full of enthusiasm, a spirit of adventure, and the knowledge gained from these pages, step into the realm of hosting with confidence. Whether you're a seasoned host or a newcomer to the world of entertaining, know that every effort you put into creating a warm, inviting space is a gift—an offering that transcends the physical aspects of the table and becomes a celebration of the shared human experience.

Here's to the laughter that echoes in your dining room, the aromas that waft from your kitchen, and the connections that blossom around your table. May your hosting adventures be filled with joy, camaraderie, and the sweet satisfaction that comes from creating moments that endure. Cheers to the art of hosting, the canvas of connection that you paint with every gathering.